Pandas

In 8 Hours

For Beginners

Learn Coding Fast

Ray Yao

About This Book

"Pandas Programming" is a textbook for high school and college students; it covers all essential Pandas language knowledge. You can learn complete primary skills of Pandas programming fast and easily.

The textbook includes a lot of practical examples for beginners and includes exercises for the college final exam, the engineer certification exam, and the job interview exam.

"Pandas Programming" is a useful textbook for beginners. The straightforward definitions, the plain examples, the elaborate explanations and the neat layout feature this helpful and educative book. You will be impressed by its distinctive and tidy writing style. Reading this book is a great enjoyment!

Note

This book is only suitable for programming beginners, high school students and college students; it is not for the experienced programmers.

Prerequisite to Learn Pandas

Before learning the Pandas, you should have basic knowledge of Python programming.

Kindle Books by Ray Yao

C# Cheat Sheet

C++ Cheat Sheet

JAVA Cheat Sheet

JavaScript Cheat Sheet

PHP MySQL Cheat Sheet

Python Cheat Sheet

Html Css Cheat Sheet

Linux Command Line

Paperback Books by Ray Yao

C# Cheat Sheet

C++ Cheat Sheet

JAVA Cheat Sheet

JavaScript Cheat Sheet

PHP MySQL Cheat Sheet

Python Cheat Sheet

Html Css Cheat Sheet

Linux Command Line

(Each Cheat Sheet contains more than 300 examples, more than 300 outputs, and more than 300 explanations.)

Table of Contents

Hour 1

Prerequisite to Learn Pandas

Before learning the Pandas, you should have basic knowledge of Python and the array, because Pandas work with Python and arrays.

What is Pandas?

Pandas is a Python-based tool that was created to complete the tasks of the data analysis. Pandas incorporates a large number of Python libraries and some standard data models, providing the necessary tools that can efficiently manipulate large data sets.

Pandas is a data analysis package for Python, originally developed by AQR Capital Management in April 2008 and became the open source in late 2009. Pandas derived its name from Panel Data and Python Data Analysis.

Pandas has a number of built-in functions and methods that allow us to work with data quickly and easily. It's a great reason that makes Python such a powerful and efficient tool for data analysis.

Pandas are used in a wide range of industries, including finance, economics, statistics, analysis and other academic and business fields.

Using Pandas, we can complete five typical steps in data processing and analysis: load, prepare, operate, model and analyze.

Pandas is a one of the Python libraries.

What Panda Is Used For?

Pandas can help us analyze complex data and draw accurate conclusions based on statistics.

Pandas can make the complex data sets clear and explicit, and make their data structures relevant and understandable.

Pandas is good for the research of data science.

Panda is used to analysis data in various fields.

Prerequisite to learn Pandas

Before you learn Pandas programming, you must have the knowledge of the Python language.

Install Pandas

1. Before installing Pandas, you need to install the latest version Python to your local computer. The Python download link is:

https://www.python.org/

2. Having downloaded the Python installer, you can install Python.

3. After installing Python, please restart your computer.

4. Test the Python. Please click:

Window System > Command Prompt > Input the following command:

C:\User\YourName>python

```
C:\Users\RAY>python
Python 3.9.4 (tags/v3.9.4:1f2e308, Apr
Type "help", "copyright", "credits" or
>>>
```

5. If you can see the Python version, it means that Pathos have installed successfully.

6. The command to install Pandas is:

```
C:\User\YourName>pip install Pandas
```

7. Please click:

Window System > Command Prompt > Input the following command:

C:\User\YourName>pip install pandas

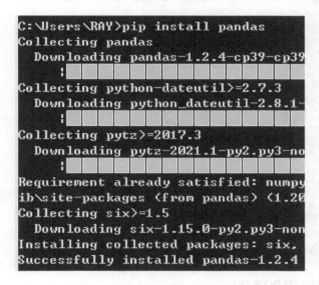

C:\Users\RAY>pip install pandas

8. After install Pandas, you can see:

```
C:\Users\RAY>pip install pandas
Collecting pandas
  Downloading pandas-1.2.4-cp39-cp39
  :
Collecting python-dateutil>=2.7.3
  Downloading python_dateutil-2.8.1-
  :
Collecting pytz>=2017.3
  Downloading pytz-2021.1-py2.py3-no
  :
Requirement already satisfied: numpy
ib\site-packages (from pandas) (1.20
Collecting six>=1.5
  Downloading six-1.15.0-py2.py3-non
Installing collected packages: six,
Successfully installed pandas-1.2.4
```

9. Congratulation! Pandas has been installed successfully!

Set Up Python Editor

We need to set up Python first so that it can work as a Pandas editor.

1. Please click:

Python3.9 > IDLE (Python 3.9 64-bit) > open the Python editor.

2. Please click:

Options > Configure IDLE > General > Open Edit Window > OK.

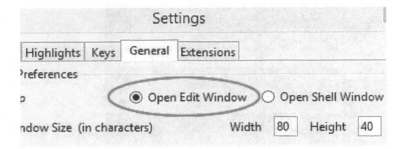

3. Restart the Python/Pandas Editor.

Congratulation! You can easily edit your Pandas program by using this editor from now on.

Import Pandas

We need to import Pandas library before doing something with Pandas programming.

There are two ways to import Pandas library.

The 1st syntax to import Pandas library is:

```
import pandas
```

Example 1.1

```
import pandas
print( pandas.__version__ )     # check Pandas version
```

Output:

0.23.4

Explanation:

"import pandas" is used to import the Pandas library.

"pandas.__version__" checks the Pandas version.

"0.23.4" is the version of Pandas library.

Import Pandas Alias

There are two ways to import Pandas library.

The 2nd syntax to import Pandas library is:

```
import pandas as pd
```

"pd" is the alias of the Pandas library.

Example 1.2

```
import pandas as pd

print( pd.__version__ )      # check Pandas version
```

Output:

0.23.4

Explanation:

"import pandas as pd" is used to import the Pandas library.

"pd" is the alias of the Pandas library.

"pd.__version__" checks the Pandas version.

"0.23.4" is the version of Pandas library.

Series

A Pandas Series is a one-dimensional array, just like a table with a single column.

The syntax to create Series is:

pd.Series(data)

Example 1.3

```
import pandas as pd

data = [ 10, 11, 12 ]

dataset = pd.Series(data)

print(dataset)     # dataset is the result of the Series
```

Output:

```
0     10
1     11
2     12
dtype: int64
```

Explanation:

"pd.Series(data)" returns a table with one column (10, 11, 12). The "0, 1, 2" is the row number. The data type is int64.

Access Series

The syntax to access Series is:

```
dataset[index]
```

Series index starts with 0 by default

Example 1.4

```
import pandas as pd

data = [ 10, 11, 12 ]

dataset = pd.Series(data)

print(dataset[0])

print(dataset[1])

print(dataset[2])
```

Output:

```
10
11
12
```

Explanation:

"dataset[index]" returns the specified value of dataset.

Create a Label

The syntax to create the label for each index is:

```
Series(data, index = ["label1", "label2", "label3"])
```

We can access Series data by its labels:

```
dataset ["label"]
```

Example 1.5

```
import pandas as pd
data = [ 10, 11, 12 ]
dataset = pd.Series(data,index = ["a", "b", "c"])
print(dataset["a"])
print(dataset["b"])
print(dataset["c"])
```

Output:

```
10
11
12
```

Explanation:

"Series(data,index = ["a", "b", "c"])" creates three labels "a, b, c" for each index. We can access the Series by labels.

Key/Value Series

The data of the Series can be a "key/value" object. This "key/value" object is just like a dictionary in Python.

```
{ key1:value1,  key2: value2,  key3:value3…}
```

Example 1.6

```
import pandas as pd

score = {"Anddy": 96, "Billy": 99, "Cindy": 98}

dataset = pd.Series(score)

print(dataset)
```

Output:

```
Anddy     96
Billy     99
Cindy     98
dtype: int64
```

Explanation:

"{"Anddy": 96, "Billy": 99, "Cindy": 98}" is a three key/value dictionary.

The keys of the dictionary become the index.

Access Series by Key

The syntax to create the key for each index is:

```
Series(data, index = ["key1", "key2", "key3"])
```

We can access the data of "key/value" Series by its key:

```
dataset["key"]    # return the value of the Series
```

Example 1.7

```
import pandas as pd

score = {"Anddy": 96, "Billy": 99, "Cindy": 98}

dataset = pd.Series(score, index = ["Billy"])

print(dataset)
```

Output:

```
Billy     99
dtype: int64
```

Explanation:

"Series(score, index = ["Billy"])" creates one key "Billy" for one index of the Series.

We can access the data of "key/value" Series by its key.

Hour 2

22

DataFrame

A Pandas DataFrame is a two-dimensional array, just like a table with rows and columns. The syntax to create a DataFrame is:

```
pd.DataFrame(data)
```

Example 2.1

```
import pandas as pd
data = {
  "Student": ["Anddy", "Billy", "Cindy"],
  "Score": [96, 99, 98]
}
dataset = pd.DataFrame(data)
print(dataset)     # dataset is the result of the DataFrame
```

Output:

```
   Student  Score
0  Anddy    96
1  Billy    99
2  Cindy    98
```

Explanation:

"pd.DataFrame(data)" creates a DataFrame, It looks like a table with rows and columns.

23

Locate the Row (1)

In a table with rows and columns, we can locate the data by the specified row. The row number starts from 0. The syntax is:

```
dataset.loc[row_number]      # using [ ]
```

loc[row_number] returns a Series date in the specified row.

Example 2.2

```
import pandas as pd
data = {
  "Student": ["Anddy", "Billy", "Cindy"],
  "Score": [96, 99, 98]
}
dataset = pd.DataFrame(data)
print(dataset.loc[1])
```

Output:

```
Student      Billy
Score           99
Name: 1, dtype: object
```

Explanation:

"**dataset.loc[1]**" locates the data in row 1.

Note: the result is a Series. "Name: 1" indicates row 1.

Locate the Row (2)

In a table with rows and columns, we can locate the data by the specified row. The row number starts from 0. The syntax is:

```
dataset.loc[[row_number]]     # using [[ ]]
```

loc[[row_number]] returns a DataFrame date in the specified row.

Example 2.3

```
import pandas as pd
data = {
  "Student": ["Anddy", "Billy", "Cindy"],
  "Score": [96, 99, 98]
}
dataset = pd.DataFrame(data)
print(dataset.loc[[1]])
```

Output:

```
   Student   Score
1   Billy      99
```

Explanation:

dataset.loc[[1]]" locates the data in row 1.

Note: the result is a DataFrame.

Set Up Index

We can set up indexes for a DataFrame, these indexes can replace the original default row numbers. The syntax is:

DataFrame(data, index = ["v1", "v2", "v3",…])

["v1", "v2", "v3",…] is the new indexes you will set up.

Example 2.4

```
import pandas as pd
data = {
  "Student": ["Anddy", "Billy", "Cindy"],
  "Score": [96, 99, 98]
}
dataset = pd.DataFrame(data, index = ["A", "B", "C"])
print(dataset)
```

Output:

```
    Student    Score
A    Anddy      96
B    Billy      99
C    Cindy      98
```

Explanation:

"index = ["A", "B", "C"]" sets up your own indexes "A, B, C".

Locate the Index

Example 2.5

```
import pandas as pd
data = {
  "Student": ["Anddy", "Billy", "Cindy"],
  "Score": [96, 99, 98]
}
dataset = pd.DataFrame(data, index = ["A", "B", "C"])
print(dataset.loc["B"])     # return a Series
print('-----------------------')
print(dataset.loc[["B"]])     # return a DataFrame
```

Output:

```
Student      Billy
Score           99
Name: B, dtype: object
-------------------------
   Student  Score
B   Billy     99
```

Explanation:

"dataset.loc["B"]" returns a Series by the index "B".

"dataset.loc[["B"]]" returns a DataFrame by the index "B".

Data File

Pandas can work with various data files, such as a CSV file, JSON file, Python dictionary file......, all these files contain tabular data, which is used for data analysis and calculation.

After we create a data file, we can save it in a specified folder, for example: C:\myData, so that we can load the file from this folder. Therefore, we can create a folder "C:\myData" beforehand, then save all data files in this folder so that the file can be loaded easily later.

Example 2.6

1. Create a folder named "myData" in C:\

2. Create a CSV file from Excel, which contains the data as follow:

Year	Anddy	Billy	Cindy	Daisy
2014	96	81	89	84
2015	91	70	92	87
2016	96	99	98	97
2017	86	91	78	69
2018	98	76	83	91
2019	71	80	92	85
2020	90	98	88	92
2021	85	72	68	93

3. Save the file named "**score.csv**" in the folder "**C:\myData**".

Read CSV File (1)

The syntax to read a CSV file is:

```
read_csv(' path\myfile.csv ')
```

Example 2.7

```
import pandas as pd
dataset = pd.read_csv('C:\myData\score.csv')
print(dataset)
```

Output:

```
    Year   Anddy   Billy   Cindy   Daisy
0   2014      96      81      89      84
1   2015      91      70      92      87
2   2016      96      99      98      97
3   2017      86      91      78      69
4   2018      98      76      83      91
5   2019      71      80      92      85
6   2020      90      98      88      92
7   2021      85      72      68      93
```

Explanation:

"read_csv('C:\myData\score.csv')" reads the file "score.csv" in the folder "C:\myData".

Read CSV File (2)

When the result will be printed, some Pandas version needs "to_string()" to print the **whole** dataframe. The syntax is:

```
print(dataset.to_string())
```

Example 2.8

```
import pandas as pd

dataset = pd.read_csv('C:\myData\score.csv')

print(dataset.to_string())     # print whole dataframe
```

Output:

```
    Year  Anddy  Billy  Cindy  Daisy
0   2014     96     81     89     84
1   2015     91     70     92     87
2   2016     96     99     98     97
3   2017     86     91     78     69
4   2018     98     76     83     91
5   2019     71     80     92     85
6   2020     90     98     88     92
7   2021     85     72     68     93
```

"**print(dataset.to_string())**" makes sure to print **whole** dataframe.

Create a JSON File

Now we can create a JSON file like this:

```json
{
 "Rosy":{
  "0":98,
  "1":85,
  "2":89
 },
 "Tomy":{
  "0":80,
  "1":78,
  "2":92
 },
 "Judy":{
  "0":74,
  "1":83,
  "2":99
 }
}
```

Save this file named **"grade.json"** in the folder **"C:\myData"**.

Read JSON File

The syntax to read a JSON file is:

```
read_json(' path\myfile.json ')
```

Example 2.9

```
import pandas as pd

dataset = pd.read_json('C:\myData\grade.json')

print(dataset)
```

Output:

```
      Rosy   Tomy   Judy
0       98     80     74
1       85     78     83
2       89     92     99
```

Explanation:

"read_json('C:\myData\grade.json')" reads the file "grade.json" in the folder "C:\myData".

(Note: If you want to know more JSON, please read the book "Xml Json Programming" by Ray Yao).

Create a Python Dictionary

Now we can create a Python dictionary like this:

```
{
  "Rosy":{
    "0":98,
    "1":85,
    "2":89
  },
  "Tomy":{
    "0":80,
    "1":78,
    "2":92
  },
  "Judy":{
    "0":74,
    "1":83,
    "2":99
  }
}
```

Save this file named **"grade.py"** in the folder **"C:\myData"**.

Read Python Dictionary

The structure of the Python dictionary is same as the structure of the JSON. "read_json()" can also read the Python dictionary.

The syntax to read a Python dictionary is:

```
read_json(' path\myfile.py ')
```

Example 2.10

```
import pandas as pd
dataset = pd.read_json('C:\myData\grade.py')
print(dataset)
```

Output:

	Rosy	Tomy	Judy
0	98	80	74
1	85	78	83
2	89	92	99

Explanation:

read_json('C:\myData\grade.py')" reads the file "grade.py" in the folder "C:\myData".

Hour 3

Embed Python Dictionary

Example 3.1

```
import pandas as pd
grade ={        # embed a Python Dictionary
 "Rosy":{
  "0":98,
  "1":85,
  "2":89
 },
 "Tomy":{
  "0":80,
  "1":78,
  "2":92
 },
 "Judy":{
  "0":74,
  "1":83,
  "2":99
 }
}
dataset = pd.DataFrame(grade)
print(dataset)
```

Output:

```
    Rosy   Tomy   Judy
0     98     80     74
1     85     78     83
2     89     92     99
```

Explanation:

A Python dictionary can be embedded into the Pandas code.

"pd.DataFrame(grade)" directly reads the data from the Python dictionary.

By the way, the structure of the Python dictionary is the same as the structure of the JSON.

Print the First 5 Rows

We can view the data in the first 5 rows. The syntax is:

```
dataset.head()   # get the data in the first 5 rows by default
```

Example 3.2

```
import pandas as pd

dataset = pd.read_csv('C:\myData\score.csv')

print(dataset.head())
```

Output:

```
   Year  Anddy  Billy  Cindy  Daisy
0  2014     96     81     89     84
1  2015     91     70     92     87
2  2016     96     99     98     97
3  2017     86     91     78     69
4  2018     98     76     83     91
```

Explanation:

"head()" gets the data in the first 5 rows by default.

Specified Rows from Head

We can view the data in the specified number of rows, starting from the head.

---
dataset.head(num)

The "num" specifies the number of rows.

Example 3.3

---
import pandas as pd

dataset = pd.read_csv('C:\myData\score.csv')

print(dataset.**head(7)**)

Output:

```
   Year  Anddy  Billy  Cindy  Daisy
0  2014     96     81     89     84
1  2015     91     70     92     87
2  2016     96     99     98     97
3  2017     86     91     78     69
4  2018     98     76     83     91
5  2019     71     80     92     85
6  2020     90     98     88     92
```

Explanation:

"head(7)" gets the data of the first 7 rows.

Print the Last 5 Rows

We can view the data in the last 5 rows. The syntax is:

```
dataset.tail()    # get the data in the last 5 rows by default
```

Example 3.4

```
import pandas as pd

dataset = pd.read_csv('C:\myData\score.csv')

print(dataset.tail())
```

Output:

	Year	Anddy	Billy	Cindy	Daisy
3	2017	86	91	78	69
4	2018	98	76	83	91
5	2019	71	80	92	85
6	2020	90	98	88	92
7	2021	85	72	68	93

Explanation:

"tail()" gets the data in the last 5 rows by default.

Specified Rows from Tail

We can view the data in the specified number of rows, starting from the tail.

```
dataset.tail(num)
```

The "num" specifies the number of rows

Example 3.5

```
import pandas as pd

dataset = pd.read_csv('C:\myData\score.csv')

print(dataset.tail(7))
```

Output:

```
   Year  Anddy  Billy  Cindy  Daisy
1  2015     91     70     92     87
2  2016     96     99     98     97
3  2017     86     91     78     69
4  2018     98     76     83     91
5  2019     71     80     92     85
6  2020     90     98     88     92
7  2021     85     72     68     93
```

Explanation:

"tail(7)" gets the data of the last 7 rows.

Information of DataFrame

We can get the information about the data set in DataFrame.

```
dataset.info()
```

Example 3.6

```
import pandas as pd

dataset = pd.read_csv('C:\myData\score.csv')

print(dataset.info())
```

Output:

```
<class 'pandas.core.frame.DataFrame'>
RangeIndex: 8 entries, 0 to 7
Data columns (total 5 columns):
 #   Column  Non-Null Count   Dtype
---  ------  --------------   -----
 0   Year    8 non-null       int64
 1   Anddy   8 non-null       int64
 2   Billy   8 non-null       int64
 3   Cindy   8 non-null       int64
 4   Daisy   8 non-null       int64
dtypes: int64(5)
memory usage: 448.0 bytes
None
```

"print(dataset.**info()**)" shows the information about the data set in the dataframe.

About the following result:

```
RangeIndex: 8 entries, 0 to 7
Data columns (total 5 columns)
```

The result tells us there 8 rows and 5 columns in the data set.

About the following result:

```
#    Column  Non-Null Count  Dtype

---  ------  --------------  -----

0    Year    8 non-null      int64
1    Anddy   8 non-null      int64
2    Billy   8 non-null      int64
3    Cindy   8 non-null      int64
4    Daisy   8 non-null      int64
```

The result tells us the names of each column, the number of the column and the data type of each value.

The result also tells us how many non-null values in the data set.

If some null values occur, it is not a good thing for data analysis; we should try to remove the rows with null value.

Null Values Occur

The rows with null values are no good for data analysis, so we should remove the rows containing null values in time.

Assume that we create a CSV file as follows:

Year	Anddy	Billy	Cindy	Daisy
2014	96	81	89	84
2015	91	70	92	87
2016	96	99	98	97
2017	86	91	78	NaN
2018	98	76	83	91
2019	NaN	80	92	85
2020	90	98	88	92
2021	85	72	68	93

Save this file named **"empty.csv"** in the folder **"C:\myData"**.

Note: the null values present in the rows of 2017 and 2019.

Remove Null Values

The syntax to remove the rows containing null value is:

```
dataset.dropna(inplace = True)
```

Example 3.7

```
import pandas as pd

dataset = pd.read_csv('C:\myData\empty.csv')

dataset.dropna( inplace = True )

print(dataset.to_string())
```

Output:

```
    Year  Anddy  Billy  Cindy  Daisy
0   2014   96.0     81     89   84.0
1   2015   91.0     70     92   87.0
2   2016   96.0     99     98   97.0
4   2018   98.0     76     83   91.0
6   2020   90.0     98     88   92.0
7   2021   85.0     72     68   93.0
```

Explanation:

"dataset.dropna()" removes the rows containing empty value.

The rows of 2017 and 2019 have been removed.

Fill in Value

We can fill in a new value in the empty cells.

```
dataset.fillna( value , inplace = True )
```

Example 3.8

```
import pandas as pd
dataset = pd.read_csv('C:\myData\empty.csv')
dataset. fillna( 95, inplace = True )
print(dataset.to_string())
```

Output:

	Year	Anddy	Billy	Cindy	Daisy
0	2014	96.0	81	89	84.0
1	2015	91.0	70	92	87.0
2	2016	96.0	99	98	97.0
3	2017	86.0	91	78	95.0
4	2018	98.0	76	83	91.0
5	2019	95.0	80	92	85.0
6	2020	90.0	98	88	92.0
7	2021	85.0	72	68	93.0

Explanation:

"fillna(95, inplace = True)" fills in the value "95" in the empty cells.

Specify Column to Fill

We can specify the column with empty value to fill in.

```
dataset[ "column_name" ]
```

Example 3.9

```
import pandas as pd
dataset = pd.read_csv('C:\myData\empty.csv')
dataset["Daisy"] . fillna( 95, inplace = True )      # fill in 95
print(dataset.to_string())
```

Output:

	Year	Anddy	Billy	Cindy	Daisy
0	2014	96.0	81	89	84.0
1	2015	91.0	70	92	87.0
2	2016	96.0	99	98	97.0
3	2017	86.0	91	78	95.0
4	2018	98.0	76	83	91.0
5	2019	NaN	80	92	85.0
6	2020	90.0	98	88	92.0
7	2021	85.0	72	68	93.0

Explanation:

"**dataset["Daisy"]**" specifies the column "Daisy" to fill in the value.

Hour 4

Fill the Average Value

Average Value: A sum is divided by the number of values.

We can get the average value in a column so as to fill in the empty cells. The syntax to get the average value is:

```
dataset["col_name"].mean()
```

Example 4.1

```
import pandas as pd
dataset = pd.read_csv('C:\myData\empty.csv')
avg = dataset["Daisy"].mean()
dataset["Daisy"].fillna( avg, inplace = True )
print(dataset.to_string())
```

Output:

```
    Year   Anddy   Billy   Cindy      Daisy
0   2014    96.0     81      89   84.000000
1   2015    91.0     70      92   87.000000
2   2016    96.0     99      98   97.000000
3   2017    86.0     91      78   89.857143
4   2018    98.0     76      83   91.000000
5   2019     NaN     80      92   85.000000
6   2020    90.0     98      88   92.000000
7   2021    85.0     72      68   93.000000
```

Explanation:

"dataset["Daisy"].mean()" gets the average value in the column "Daisy". The average value is 89.857143.

Fill the Middle Value

Middle Value: A mid value after all values are sorted.

We can get the middle value in a column so as to fill in the empty cells. The syntax to get the middle value is:

```
dataset["col_name"].median()
```

Example 4.2

```
import pandas as pd
dataset = pd.read_csv('C:\myData\empty.csv')
mid = dataset["Anddy"].median()
dataset["Anddy"] . fillna( mid, inplace = True )
print(dataset.to_string())
```

Output:

	Year	Anddy	Billy	Cindy	Daisy
0	2014	96.0	81	89	84.0
1	2015	91.0	70	92	87.0
2	2016	96.0	99	98	97.0
3	2017	86.0	91	78	NaN
4	2018	98.0	76	83	91.0
5	2019	91.0	80	92	85.0
6	2020	90.0	98	88	92.0
7	2021	85.0	72	68	93.0

Explanation:

"dataset["Anddy"].median()" gets the middle value in the column "Anddy". The middle value is 91.0.

Fill the Most Hot Value

Hot Value: A value appears most frequently. We can get the hot value in a column so as to fill in the empty cells. The syntax is:

```
dataset["col_name"].mode()[0]     # [0] means a single value
```

Example 4.3

```
import pandas as pd
dataset = pd.read_csv('C:\myData\empty.csv')
hot = dataset["Anddy"].mode()[0]
dataset["Anddy"] . fillna( hot, inplace = True )
print(dataset.to_string())
```

Output:

```
    Year   Anddy   Billy   Cindy   Daisy
0   2014    96.0      81      89    84.0
1   2015    91.0      70      92    87.0
2   2016    96.0      99      98    97.0
3   2017    86.0      91      78     NaN
4   2018    98.0      76      83    91.0
5   2019    96.0      80      92    85.0
6   2020    90.0      98      88    92.0
7   2021    85.0      72      68    93.0
```

Explanation:

"**dataset["Anddy"].mode()[0]**" gets the hot value appearing most frequently in the column "Anddy". "96" appears most frequently.

Wrong Formats Occur

The datetime with wrong format values are no good for data analysis, so we should correct the wrong format values in time.

Assume that we create a CSV file as follows:

Date	Anddy	Billy	Cindy	Daisy
'2014/12/10'	96	81	89	84
'2015/12/11'	91	70	92	87
'2016/12/12'	96	99	98	97
20171213	86	91	78	69
'2018/12/14'	98	76	83	91
'2019/12/15'	71	80	92	85
20201216	90	98	88	92
'2021/12/17'	85	72	68	93

Save this file named "**wrong.csv**" in the folder "**C:\myData**".

Note: the wrong format values present in the column "Date". They are "20171213" and "20201216".

Correct Wrong Format

The syntax to correct the wrong format of the datetime is:

```
to_datetime(dataset['col_name'])
```

Example 4.4

```
import pandas as pd

dataset = pd.read_csv('C:\myData\wrong.csv')

dataset['Date'] = pd.to_datetime(dataset['Date'])

print(dataset.to_string())
```

Output:

```
        Date    Anddy   Billy   Cindy   Daisy
0   2014-12-10     96      81      89      84
1   2015-12-11     91      70      92      87
2   2016-12-12     96      99      98      97
3   2017-12-13     86      91      78      69
4   2018-12-14     98      76      83      91
5   2019-12-15     71      80      92      85
6   2020-12-16     90      98      88      92
7   2021-12-17     85      72      68      93
```

Explanation:

"to_datetime(dataset['Date'])" corrects the datetime format in the column "Date". The datetime in row3 & row6 has been corrected.

Incorrect Data Occur

The incorrect data are no good for data analysis, so we should remove the incorrect data in time.

Assume that we create a CSV file as follows:

Date	Anddy	Billy	Cindy	Daisy
'2014/12/10'	96	81	89	84
'2015/12/11'	91	70	92	87
'2016/12/12'	96	**199**	98	97
'2017/12/13'	86	91	78	69
'2018/12/14'	98	76	83	91
'2019/12/15'	71	80	92	85
'2020/12/16'	90	**0.98**	88	92
'2021/12/17'	85	72	68	93

Save this file named **"incorrect.csv"** in the folder **"C:\myData"**.

Note: the incorrect data appear in the column "Billy". They are "199" and "0.98".

Remove Incorrect Data

The syntax to remove the specified row is:

```
dataset.drop(row, inplace = True)
```

Example 4.5

```
import pandas as pd

dataset = pd.read_csv('C:\myData\incorrect.csv')

for row in dataset.index:      # loop through all rows

  if dataset.loc[row, "Billy"] > 100:      # if the score > 100

    dataset.drop(row, inplace = True)

print(dataset.to_string())
```

Output:

```
        Date    Anddy  Billy  Cindy  Daisy
0   '2014/12/10'    96  81.00     89     84
1   '2015/12/11'    91  70.00     92     87
3   '2017/12/13'    86  91.00     78     69
4   '2018/12/14'    98  76.00     83     91
5   '2019/12/15'    71  80.00     92     85
6   '2020/12/16'    90   0.98     88     92
7   '2021/12/17'    85  72.00     68     93
```

Explanation:

"dataset.drop(row, inplace = True)" removes the row containing the incorrect data (score> 100).

Modify Incorrect Data (1)

The syntax to modify the data with the specified value is:

```
dataset.loc[row, "col_name"] = specified_value
```

Example 4.6

```
import pandas as pd

dataset = pd.read_csv('C:\myData\incorrect.csv')

for row in dataset.index:      # loop through all rows

  if dataset.loc[row, "Billy"] < 1:      # if the score < 1

    dataset.loc[row, "Billy"] = 98      # specify 98

print(dataset.to_string())
```

Output:

	Date	Anddy	Billy	Cindy	Daisy
0	'2014/12/10'	96	81.0	89	84
1	'2015/12/11'	91	70.0	92	87
2	'2016/12/12'	96	199.0	98	97
3	'2017/12/13'	86	91.0	78	69
4	'2018/12/14'	98	76.0	83	91
5	'2019/12/15'	71	80.0	92	85
6	'2020/12/16'	90	98.0	88	92
7	'2021/12/17'	85	72.0	68	93

Explanation:

"dataset.loc[row, "Billy"] = 98" modifies the incorrect data (score<1) with a specified value "98".

Modify Incorrect Data (2)

The syntax to modify the incorrect data with a mid value is:

```
dataset.loc[row, "col_name"] = mid_value
```

Example 4.7

```
import pandas as pd

dataset = pd.read_csv('C:\myData\incorrect.csv')

mid = dataset["Billy"].median()    # get a mid value

for row in dataset.index:    # loop through all rows

  if dataset.loc[row, "Billy"] < 1:    # if score < 1

    dataset.loc[row, "Billy"] = mid    # modify with a mid value

print(dataset.to_string())
```

Output:

```
            Date   Anddy   Billy   Cindy   Daisy
0    '2014/12/10'     96    81.0      89      84
1    '2015/12/11'     91    70.0      92      87
2    '2016/12/12'     96   199.0      98      97
3    '2017/12/13'     86    91.0      78      69
4    '2018/12/14'     98    76.0      83      91
5    '2019/12/15'     71    80.0      92      85
6    '2020/12/16'     90    78.0      88      92
7    '2021/12/17'     85    72.0      68      93
```

Explanation:

"**loc[row, "Billy"] = mid**" modifies the incorrect data (score<1) with a mid value "78.0".

Duplicate Data

The duplicate data are no good for data analysis, so we should remove the row with duplicate data in time.

Assume that we create a CSV file as follows:

Date	Anddy	Billy	Cindy	Daisy
'2014/12/10'	96	81	89	84
'2015/12/11'	91	70	92	87
'2016/12/12'	96	99	98	97
'2017/12/13'	86	91	78	69
'2018/12/14'	**98**	**76**	**83**	**91**
'2018/12/14'	**98**	**76**	**83**	**91**
'2019/12/15'	71	80	92	85
'2020/12/16'	90	98	88	92
'2021/12/17'	85	72	68	93

Save this file named **"duplicate.csv"** in the folder **"C:\myData"**.

Note: the duplicate data present in the row '2018/12/14'.

Find Duplicate Data

The syntax to find the duplicate date is:

```
dataset.duplicated()
```

If return true, it means that a duplicate data occurs.

Example 4.8

```
import pandas as pd

dataset = pd.read_csv('C:\myData\duplicate.csv')

print(dataset.duplicated())
```

Output:

```
0     False
1     False
2     False
3     False
4     False
5      True
6     False
7     False
8     False
dtype: bool
```

Explanation:

"**duplicated())**" finds the duplicate data in a specified file. If the result is true, it means the data is duplicated. The row 5 containing '2018/12/14' is the duplicated data.

Remove Duplicate Data

The syntax to remove the duplicate data is:

```
dataset.drop_duplicates(inplace = True)
```

Example 4.9

```
import pandas as pd

dataset = pd.read_csv('C:\myData\duplicate.csv')

dataset.drop_duplicates(inplace = True)

print(dataset.to_string())
```

Output:

```
        Date     Anddy  Billy  Cindy  Daisy
0  '2014/12/10'     96     81     89     84
1  '2015/12/11'     91     70     92     87
2  '2016/12/12'     96     99     98     97
3  '2017/12/13'     86     91     78     69
4  '2018/12/14'     98     76     83     91
6  '2019/12/15'     71     80     92     85
7  '2020/12/16'     90     98     88     92
8  '2021/12/17'     85     72     68     93
```

Explanation:

"drop_duplicates(inplace = True)" has removed the row containing the duplicated data **"'2018/12/14'"**.

Hour 5

Data Correlation

Data Correlation is very import for data analysis. The each factor of the data always affects and interact each other. Through the relationship of the each data, we can draw some scientific conclusions, obtain some accurate judgments.

Assume we have a table about the car's data as follows:

Car Age	Price	Power	Oil Wear
3	50000	206	6
6	31000	120	11
5	40000	135	9
9	18000	50	15
7	26000	102	13
4	45000	160	8
8	19000	78	14
2	55000	220	5

Save the file named "**car.csv**" in the folder "**C:\myData**".

Get Data Correlation

We can get the data's correlation of each column. The syntax is:

```
dataset.corr()
```

Example 5.1

```
import pandas as pd
dataset = pd.read_csv('C:\myData\car.csv')
print(dataset.corr())
```

Output:

```
              Car Age      Price      Power   Oil Wear

Car Age      1.000000  -0.993297  -0.991761   0.995504

Price       -0.993297   1.000000   0.979124  -0.996034

Power       -0.991761   0.979124   1.000000  -0.986401

Oil Wear     0.995504  -0.996034  -0.986401   1.000000
```

Explanation:

"**dataset.corr()**" returns the correlation between each column.

The values of correlation always appear in the range from -1 to 1.

Let's view the chart about the data correlation as follows:

Data Correlation Chart:

+1.0 Perfect Correlation. It means:

If one value increases, another value will increase.

If one value decreases, another value will decrease.

-1.0 Perfect Correlation. It means:

If one value increases, another value will decrease.

If one value decreases, another value will increase.

From +0.6 to +0.9 Good Correlation. It means:

If one value increases, another value will increase.

If one value decreases, another value will decrease.

From -0.6 to -0.9 Good Correlation. It means:

If one value increases, another value will decrease.

If one value decreases, another value will increase.

From +0.1 to +0.5 Bad Correlation. It means:

If one value increases, another value may not increase.

If one value decreases, another value may not decrease.

From -0.1 to -0.5 Bad Correlation. It means:

If one value increases, another value may not decrease.

If one value decreases, another value may not increase.

0 No Correlation. It means:

The increase or decrease of the one value has no any correlation with another value.

Series Random Number

Series random number ranges from -1 to +1.

The syntax to create some random numbers in Series is:

```
Series(np.random.randn(num))
```

"num" specifies how many random numbers should generate.

Example 5.2

```
import pandas as pd
import numpy as np      # numpy is another Python library
dataset = pd.Series(np.random.randn(5))
print (dataset)
```

Output:

```
0    -0.307806
1    -0.447883
2     1.543413
3     1.221386
4    -0.767047
dtype: float64
```

Explanation:

"Series(np.random.randn(5))" generates 5 random numbers in the series.

"numpy" library is used to work with arrays.

Check Series Empty

We check whether the Series is empty. The syntax is:

```
dataset.empty
```

If returns true, the Series is empty, and vice verse.

Example 5.3

```
import pandas as pd

import numpy as np

dataset = pd.Series(np.random.randn(5))

# generate 5 random numbers

print ("Is the Series empty?")

print (dataset.empty)
```

Output:

```
Is the Series empty?
False
```

Explanation:

"**dataset.empty**" checks whether the Series is empty.

"False" means that the Series is not empty.

Check Series Size

The syntax to check the Series size is:

```
dataset.size
```

Example 5.4

```
import pandas as pd

import numpy as np

dataset = pd.Series(np.random.randn(5))

print ("The size of the Series is:")

print (dataset.size)
```

Output:

The size of the Series is:

5

Explanation:

"**dataset.size**" checks the size of a Series.

"5" means that the Series has five values.

Array Values of Series

We can show the Series data in the way of array values.

The syntax is as follows:

```
dataset.values     # return an array
```

Example 5.5

```
import pandas as pd

import numpy as np

dataset = pd.Series(np.random.randn(5))

print ("The array value of the series is:")

print (dataset.values)
```

Output:

The array values of the series are:

[-1.37514714 -0.82150901 0.03638524 -0.67271975 0.37295707]

Explanation:

"**dataset.values**" returns the array values of the Series.

The result of the data is an array.

Transpose a DataFrame

"Transpose" means that the rows and the columns of the DataFrame can be exchanged. The original rows become new columns, the original columns become new rows.

The syntax to transpose the data of a DataFrame is:

```
dataset.T
```

Let's take the "grade.py" as an example.

Example 5.6

```
import pandas as pd

dataset = pd.read_json('C:\myData\grade.py')

print ("The original date of the Dataframe is:")

print (dataset)

print ('---------------------------------------')

print ("The transposed date of the DataFrame is:")

print (dataset.T)     # transpose a Dataframe
```

69

The original date of the Dataframe is:

	Rosy	Tomy	Judy
0	98	80	74
1	85	78	83
2	89	92	99

The transposed date of the DataFrame is:

	0	1	2
Rosy	98	85	89
Tomy	80	78	92
Judy	74	83	99

Explanation:

"**dataset.T**" transposes the data of the dataframe.

We can see the exchange between rows and columns.

Check Data Type

The syntax to check the data type of a DataFrame is:

```
dataset. Dtypes
```

Example 5.7

```python
import pandas as pd

data = {

  "Student": ["Anddy", "Billy", "Cindy"],

  "Score": [96, 99, 98],

  "Average": [95.38, 98.23, 98.12],

}

dataset = pd.DataFrame(data)

print(dataset. Dtypes)
```

Output:

```
Student       object
Score          int64
Average      float64
dtype: object
```

Explanation:

"dataset. Dtypes" checks the data type of each column in a DataFrame.

71

Array Values of DataFrame

We can show the DataFrame data in the way of array values.

The syntax is as follows:

```
dataset.values      # return an array
```

Example 5.8

```
import pandas as pd

dataset = pd.read_csv('C:\myData\score.csv')

print (dataset.values)
```

Output:

```
[[2014    96    81    89    84]
 [2015    91    70    92    87]
 [2016    96    99    98    97]
 [2017    86    91    78    69]
 [2018    98    76    83    91]
 [2019    71    80    92    85]
 [2020    90    98    88    92]
 [2021    85    72    68    93]]
```

Explanation:

"dataset.values" returns the array values of the DataFrame.

The result of the data is a 2-d array.

Size, Ndim, Shape

The syntax to get the information of a DataFrame is:

```
dataset.size     # return the number of the values

dataset.ndim     # return the number of the dimensions

dataset.shape    # return the number of the rows and columns
```

Example 5.9

```
import pandas as pd

dataset = pd.read_csv('C:\myData\score.csv')

print(dataset.size)

print(dataset.ndim)

print(dataset.shape)
```

Output:

```
40
2
 (8, 5)
```

Explanation:

"40" means that the DataFrame has 40 values.

"2" means that the DataFrame is a 2-d dataset.

(8, 5) means that the DataFrame has 8 rows and 5 columns.

Hour 6

The Sum of Each Column

We can get the sum of each column's value. The syntax is:

```
dataset.sum()
```

Example 6.1

```
import pandas as pd

dataset = pd.read_json('C:\myData\grade.py')

print (dataset)

print (dataset.sum())
```

Output:

```
     Rosy   Tomy   Judy
0      98     80     74
1      85     78     83
2      89     92     99
Rosy        272
Tomy        250
Judy        256
dtype: int64
```

Explanation:

"**dataset.sum()**" returns the sum of each column's value.

The Prod of Each Column

We can get the product of each column's value. The syntax is:

dataset.prod()

Example 6.2

```
import pandas as pd

dataset = pd.read_json('C:\myData\grade.py')

print (dataset)

print (dataset.prod())
```

Output:

```
      Rosy    Tomy    Judy
0       98      80      74
1       85      78      83
2       89      92      99
Rosy       741370
Tomy       574080
Judy       608058
dtype: int64
```

Explanation:

"dataset.prod()" returns the product of each column's value.

76

The Maximum Values

We can get the maximum values of each column. The syntax is:

```
dataset.max()
```

Example 6.3

```
import pandas as pd

dataset = pd.read_json('C:\myData\grade.py')

print (dataset)

print (dataset.max())
```

Output:

```
     Rosy   Tomy   Judy
0      98     80     74
1      85     78     83
2      89     92     99
Rosy        98
Tomy        92
Judy        99
dtype: int64
```

Explanation:

dataset.max()" returns the maximum values of each column.

The Minimum Values

We can get the minimum values of each column. The syntax is:

```
dataset.min()
```

Example 6.4

```
import pandas as pd

dataset = pd.read_json('C:\myData\grade.py')

print (dataset)

print (dataset.min())
```

Output:

```
     Rosy    Tomy    Judy
0      98      80      74
1      85      78      83
2      89      92      99
Rosy      85
Tomy      78
Judy      74
dtype: int64
```

Explanation:

"dataset.min()" returns the minimum values of each column.

Standard Deviation

Standard Deviation describes the average distance by which each data deviates from the mean value. The larger the standard deviation, the more these data deviate from the mean value, and vice versa. (Please reference other related books.)

The syntax to get the standard deviation is:

```
dataset.std()
```

Example 6.5

```
import pandas as pd
dataset = pd.read_json('C:\myData\grade.py')
print (dataset)
print (dataset.std())
```

Output:

```
      Rosy   Tomy   Judy
0       98     80     74
1       85     78     83
2       89     92     99
Rosy         6.658328
Tomy         7.571878
Judy        12.662280
dtype: float64
```

Explanation:

"dataset.std()" returns the standard deviation of each column.

79

Count How Many Rows

We can count how many rows in a DataFrame. The syntax is:

```
dataset.count()
```

Example 6.6

```
import pandas as pd

dataset = pd.read_json('C:\myData\grade.py')

print (dataset)

print (dataset.count())
```

Output:

```
     Rosy    Tomy    Judy
0      98      80      74
1      85      78      83
2      89      92      99
Rosy      3
Tomy      3
Judy      3
dtype: int64
```

Explanation:

"dataset.count()" returns the number of rows in the DataFrame.

80

The DataFrame Description

"The DataFrame Description" means that an information about the DataFrame, such as the count, mean, std, max, min…

```
dataset.describe()
```

Example 6.7

```
import pandas as pd

dataset = pd.read_json('C:\myData\grade.py')

print (dataset)

print (dataset.describe())
```

Output:

```
     Rosy    Tomy    Judy
0      98      80      74
1      85      78      83
2      89      92      99
              Rosy         Tomy          Judy
count     3.000000     3.000000      3.000000
mean     90.666667    83.333333     85.333333
std       6.658328     7.571878     12.662280
min      85.000000    78.000000     74.000000
25%      87.000000    79.000000     78.500000
50%      89.000000    80.000000     83.000000
75%      93.500000    86.000000     91.000000
max      98.000000    92.000000     99.000000
```

Explanation:

"dataset.describe()" displays the information of the DataFrame.

Case Conversion

The syntax of case conversion is as follows:

```
str.lower()    # convert all strings into lower case
str.upper()    # convert all strings into upper case
```

Example 6.8

```
import pandas as pd

import numpy as np

dataset = pd.Series(['Anddy', 'Billy', 'Cindy', 'Daisy'])

print (dataset.str.lower())

print (dataset.str.upper())
```

Output:

```
0       anddy
1       billy
2       cindy
3       daisy
dtype: object
0       ANDDY
1       BILLY
2       CINDY
3       DAISY
dtype: object
```

Output:

"**str.lower()**" converts the string in dataset into lower case.

"**str.upper()**" converts the string in dataset into upper case.

String Length

The string length means the number of the characters of each string. The syntax to get the string length is:

```
str.len()
```

Example 6.9

```
import pandas as pd
dataset = pd.Series(['Antelope', 'Buffalo', 'Camel', 'Deer'])
print(dataset.str.len())
```

Output:

```
0    8
1    7
2    5
3    4
dtype: int64
```

Explanation:

"str.len()" returns the length of each string.

" 0   8 " means that the string in the index 0 has 8 characters

...... and so on.

Number of Characters

We can get the number of the characters of a specified character in a string. The syntax to get the number of characters is:

```
str.count(character)
```

Example 6.10

```
import pandas as pd

dataset = pd.Series(['Antelope', 'Buffalo', 'Camel', 'Deer'])

print(dataset.str.count('e'))
```

Output:

```
0    2
1    0
2    1
3    2
dtype: int64
```

Explanation:

"**str.count('e')**" counts the number of character "e" in each string.

" 0   2 " means that the string in the index 0 has 2 characters "e".

...... and so on.

Find the Index

The syntax to find the index of a specified character is:

```
str.find('character')
```

Example 6.11

```
import pandas as pd
dataset = pd.Series(['Antelope', 'Buffalo', 'Camel', 'Deer'])
print(dataset.str.find('e'))
```

Output:

```
0     3
1    -1
2     3
3     1
dtype: int64
```

Explanation:

"str.find('e')" finds the index of the specified character "e" in each string.

" 0   3 " means that the index of the "e" is "3" in the "Antelope".

" 1 -1 " means that "Buffalo" has no "e".

…… and so on.

Other String Functions

strip() Remove space of each string	
split() Split every string using the specified delimiter.	
cat() Concatenate strings	
contains(character) Check whether the string contains the specified character.	
replace(x, y) Replace x with y	
repeat(number) repeat to run according to the specified number of times	
startswith(character) Return true if the string starts with the specified character	
endswith(character) Return true if the string ends with the specified character	
swapcase() Convert the character case	
islower() Check whether all characters are lower case	
isupper() Check whether all characters are upper case	
isnumeric() Check whether all characters are numbers	

Hour 7

Row Name & Column Name

We can customize all row names and all column names.

```
index=[row1_name, row2_name, row3_name,…]

columns=[col1_name, col2_name, col3_name,…]
```

Example 7.1   (Create a dataframe with 6x4 random numbers)

```
import pandas as pd
import numpy as np
dataset=pd.DataFrame(np.random.randn(6,4),
index=[3,5,2,6,1,4],columns=['Beck', 'Davy', 'Anna', 'Cary'])
print (dataset)
```

Output:

```
      Beck       Davy       Anna       Cary
3  1.482356  -1.273772   0.417523  -0.711904
5  1.280218   0.595535  -2.319749  -1.059223
2 -0.074116  -1.126863   0.970934   1.642102
6  1.201247  -0.924285   0.241328  -1.245626
1  0.908684   1.093804  -0.383423   0.506746
4 -0.501217  -0.403617   0.456819  -0.384363
```

Explanation:

"index=[3,5,2,5,1,4]" customizes each row name as 3,5,2,6,1,4.

"columns=['Beck', 'Davy', 'Anna', 'Cary']" customizes each column name as 'Beck', 'Davy', 'Anna', 'Cary'.

Sort by Row Names

We can sort a dataframe according to rows. The syntax is:

```
dataset.sort_index(axis=0)
```

Example 7.2

```
import pandas as pd

import numpy as np

dataset=pd.DataFrame(np.random.randn(6,4),

index=[3,5,2,6,1,4],columns=['Beck', 'Davy', 'Anna', 'Cary'])

result=dataset.sort_index(axis=0)

print (result)
```

Output:

```
        Beck       Davy       Anna       Cary
1   0.700162  -0.256875  -2.170812   0.101197
2  -0.302549   0.429332  -0.385746   1.661160
3   2.610807   1.995347  -0.252548  -1.809958
4   0.622751  -0.684494   0.742842  -0.095861
5   1.083048   1.500929   0.135688   0.829634
6  -0.994862  -1.482579  -0.379976   0.086631
```

Explanation:

"dataset.sort_index(axis=0)" sorts the dataframe by rows.

The rows order in output is: 1,2,3,4,5,6.

Sort by Column Names

We can sort a dataframe according to columns. The syntax is:

```
dataset.sort_index(axis=1)
```

Example 7.3

```
import pandas as pd

import numpy as np

dataset=pd.DataFrame(np.random.randn(6,4),

index=[3,5,2,6,1,4],columns=['Beck', 'Davy', 'Anna', 'Cary'])

result=dataset.sort_index(axis=1)

print (result)
```

Output:

```
        Anna       Beck       Cary       Davy
3   0.853116   0.612809  -0.823322   0.271361
5   1.167714   1.347619   1.384097   0.441532
2   0.035531  -0.449383   0.246522   1.479868
6  -0.134057  -1.437019  -0.851346  -0.604714
1   1.488239   0.776598   0.336811   0.595531
4   1.023263  -2.005235  -1.302457   0.917117
```

Explanation:

"dataset.sort_index(axis=1)" sorts the dataframe by columns.

The column order in output is: Anna, Beck, Cary, Davy.

Sort in Ascending Order

We can sort a dataframe by the index in ascending order.

---

dataset.sort_index(ascending=True)

Example 7.4

```
import pandas as pd

import numpy as np

dataset=pd.DataFrame(np.random.randn(6,4),

index=[3,5,2,6,1,4],columns=['Beck', 'Davy', 'Anna', 'Cary'])

result=dataset.sort_index(ascending=True)

print (result)
```

Output:

```
       Beck       Davy       Anna       Cary
1   0.950626  -1.580885   0.879199  -0.695477
2  -1.530600   0.136803   1.252210   1.369068
3   0.643664  -0.535462   0.716861  -1.660582
4   1.072985   0.881788  -0.741638   0.643742
5  -0.111353  -0.497658   0.535674   0.582772
6   0.438234  -0.682980   0.596169  -0.821808
```

Explanation:

"dataset.sort_index(ascending=True)" sorts the dataframe in ascending order.

The index order in output is: 1,2,3,4,5,6.

Sort in Descending Order

We can sort a dataframe by the index in descending order.

```
dataset.sort_index(ascending=False)
```

Example 7.5

```
import pandas as pd

import numpy as np

dataset=pd.DataFrame(np.random.randn(6,4),

index=[3,5,2,6,1,4],columns=['Beck', 'Davy', 'Anna', 'Cary'])

result=dataset.sort_index(ascending=False)

print (result)
```

Output:

```
        Beck       Davy       Anna       Cary
6   0.093467    0.183661   1.043429  -0.092537
5   1.051840   -0.811169   0.961223   0.481033
4  -0.441854    0.529363  -1.726113  -1.103023
3  -0.141013   -0.810974  -0.402111  -1.097659
2  -1.586867   -0.121410   0.827747  -0.891564
1   0.807871    0.688555  -1.081628   0.335379
```

Explanation:

"dataset.sort_index(ascending=False)" sorts the dataframe in descending order.

The index order in output is: 6,5,4,3,2,1.

Sort Vales by Column

The syntax to sort values by the specified column is:

```
dataset.sort_values(by=['col_name'])
```

Only the specified column can be sorted at one time.

Example 7.6

```
import pandas as pd

import numpy as np

dataset=pd.DataFrame(np.random.randn(6,4),

index=[3,5,2,6,1,4],columns=['Beck', 'Davy', 'Anna', 'Cary'])

result=dataset.sort_values(by=['Davy'])

print (result)
```

Output:

```
        Beck       Davy       Anna       Cary
6   0.621479  -1.006479   1.119580  -0.474335
3  -0.044795  -0.304317   1.719916  -1.306416
5   1.529755  -0.158538   0.112531  -1.917531
2   0.936668   0.041911  -1.328495  -0.750058
4  -0.368573   0.103344  -0.531743   1.285022
1   0.612415   1.016416   0.996004  -0.303717
```

Explanation:

".**sort_values(by=['Davy'])**" sorts the values in the specified column "Davy". The order of Davy's values is from small to large.

Rename Rows & Columns

We can rename all rows and columns in the dataframe.

The syntax to rename the rows and columns is:

```
rename(index={oldName:newName}, columns={oldName:newName}
```

Example 7.7

```python
import pandas as pd

import numpy as np

dataset = pd.DataFrame(np.random.randn(6,4),

index=[3,5,2,6,1,4],

columns=['Beck', 'Davy', 'Anna', 'Cary'])

print ('The original dataframe is:')

print (dataset)

print (' ')

print ("After renaming the rows and columns:")

print (dataset.rename(index={1 : 'a', 2 : 'b', 3 : 'c', 4 : 'd', 5 : 'e', 6 : 'f'},

columns={'Beck' : 'c1', 'Davy' : 'c2', 'Anna' : 'c3', 'Cary' : 'c4'}))
```

Output:

```
The original dataframe is:
      Beck      Davy      Anna      Cary
3  1.340482  1.768661  0.678216  0.446117
5 -0.087325  1.255494 -1.546561 -0.013793
2  0.558010 -1.483279 -0.214741 -1.029081
6 -0.193743  0.162661  1.201756 -1.587431
1  0.999177 -1.546489 -2.020612 -1.961596
4  0.923795 -0.311860  2.044183  1.747950

After renaming the rows and columns:
        c1        c2        c3        c4
c  1.340482  1.768661  0.678216  0.446117
e -0.087325  1.255494 -1.546561 -0.013793
b  0.558010 -1.483279 -0.214741 -1.029081
f -0.193743  0.162661  1.201756 -1.587431
a  0.999177 -1.546489 -2.020612 -1.961596
d  0.923795 -0.311860  2.044183  1.747950
```

Explanation:

"dataset.rename(index={1 : 'a', 2 : 'b', 3 : 'c', 4 : 'd', 5 : 'e', 6 : 'f'})" renames the rows.

"dataset.rename(columns={'Beck' : 'c1', 'Davy' : 'c2', 'Anna' : 'c3', 'Cary' : 'c4'})" renames the columns.

Iterate Over DataFrame (1)

We can access all values by iterating over the dataframe.

The syntax to iterate over a dataframe is:

```
for row, col in dataset.iterrows():
```

"iterrows()" will make the result grouped by row name:

Its result format looks like this:

```
row_name
col_name          value
```

Example 7.8

```
import pandas as pd

import numpy as np

dataset = pd.DataFrame(np.random.randn(3,4),

index=['r1','r2','r3'],     # define three row names

columns=['c1','c2','c3','c4'])   # define four col names

for row, col in dataset.iterrows():

   print (row, col)
```

Output:

```
r1
c1    -0.717379
c2    -0.688867
c3     1.346617
Name: r1, dtype: float64
r2
c1    -1.311421
c2     0.081984
c3    -0.554583
Name: r2, dtype: float64
r3
c1     0.346595
c2     0.448194
c3     0.560816
Name: r3, dtype: float64
r4
c1     0.279594
c2    -0.463274
c3     0.171223
Name: c4, dtype: float64
```

Explanation:

"for key,value in dataset.iterrows():" iterates over the dataframe.

"iterrows()" makes the result grouped by row name:

Its result format looks like this:

```
row_name
col_name        value
```

Iterate Over DataFrame (2)

We can access all values by iterating over the dataframe.

The syntax to iterate over a dataframe is:

```
for row, col in dataset.iteritems():
```

"iteritems()" will make the result grouped by column name:

Its result format looks like this:

```
col_name
row_name          value
```

Example 7.9

```python
import pandas as pd

import numpy as np

dataset = pd.DataFrame(np.random.randn(3,4),

index=['r1','r2','r3'],     # define three row names

columns=['c1','c2','c3','c4'])    # define four col names

for row, col in dataset.iteritems():

    print (row, col)
```

```
c1
r1    -0.717379
r2    -0.688867
r3     1.346617
Name: c1, dtype: float64
c2
r1    -1.311421
r2     0.081984
r3    -0.554583
Name: c2, dtype: float64
c3
r1     0.346595
r2     0.448194
r3     0.560816
Name: c3, dtype: float64
c4
r1     0.279594
r2    -0.463274
r3     0.171223
Name: c4, dtype: float64
```

Explanation:

"for key,value in dataset.iteritems():" iterates over the dataframe.

"iteritems()" makes the result grouped by column name.

Its result format looks like this:

```
col_name
row_name         value
```

Hour 8

Iterate Over DataFrame (3)

We can access all values by iterating over the dataframe.

The syntax to iterate over a dataframe is:

```
for result in dataset.itertuples():
```

"itertuples()" will make the result grouped by "Pandas" keyword.

Its result format looks like this:

```
Pandas(index='row_name1', col_name1='value1')
Pandas(index='row_name2', col_name2='value2')
```

Example 8.1

```
import pandas as pd
import numpy as np
dataset = pd.DataFrame(np.random.randn(3,4),
index=['r1','r2','r3'],     # define three row names
columns=['c1','c2','c3','c4'])     # define four col names
for result in dataset.itertuples():
  print (result)
```

Output:

```
Pandas(Index='r1', c1=-1.5469058426717606,
c2=0.8213502554558779, c3=-0.3836745990866013, c4=-
0.37688452243961296)

Pandas(Index='r2', c1=0.16355712356054525,
c2=1.5319072143232761, c3=0.5042198965834229,
c4=0.980905520823645)

Pandas(Index='r3', c1=0.696818194245236,
c2=0.5583047363929496, c3=0.0512532652029395, c4=-
0.17503896559077425)
```

Explanation:

"for result in dataset.itertuples():" iterates over the dataframe.

"itertuples()" makes the result grouped by "Pandas" keyword.

Its result format looks like this:

```
Pandas(index='row_name1', col_name1='value1')
Pandas(index='row_name2', col_name2='value2')
......
```

Get Range of Regular Dates

The syntax to get the range of regular dates is:

```
date_range('yyyy/mm/dd', periods=num)
```

"periods=num" specifies the number of the dates

Example 8.2

```
import pandas as pd

result = pd.date_range('2018/06/15', periods=6)

print(result)
```

Output:

```
DatetimeIndex(['2018-06-15', '2018-06-16', '2018-06-
17', '2018-06-18', '2018-06-19', '2018-06-20'],
dtype='datetime64[ns]', freq='D')
```

Explanation:

"date_range('2018/06/15', periods=6)" returns the range of regular dates beginning from "2016/06/15", including 6 days.

Get Range of Business Dates

The syntax to get the range of business dates is:

```
bdate_range('yyyy/mm/dd', periods=num)
```

"periods=num" specifies the number of the dates

Business dates do not include Saturday and Sunday.

Example 8.3

```
import pandas as pd

result = pd.bdate_range('2018/06/15', periods=6)

print(result)
```

Output:

```
DatetimeIndex(['2018-06-15', '2018-06-18', '2018-06-
19', '2018-06-20', '2018-06-21', '2018-06-22'],
dtype='datetime64[ns]', freq='B')
```

Explanation:

"bdate_range('2018/06/15', periods=6)" returns the range of business dates beginning from "2016/06/15", including 6 days.

Business dates do not include Saturday and Sunday.

Get Range of Weekends

The syntax to get the range of every weekend is:

```
date_range('yyyy/mm/dd', periods=num, freq='W')
```

"periods=num" specifies the number of the weeks

'freq='W'" specifies the every weekend.

Example 8.4

```
import pandas as pd
result = pd.date_range('2018/06/15', periods=6, freq='W')
print(result)
```

Output:

```
DatetimeIndex(['2018-06-17', '2018-06-24', '2018-07-
01', '2018-07-08', '2018-07-15', '2018-07-22'],
dtype='datetime64[ns]', freq='W-SUN')
```

Explanation:

"date_range('2018/06/15', periods=6, freq='W')" returns every weekend starting from "2018/06/15", including 6 weekends.

Get Range of Month End

The syntax to get the range of every month end is:

```
date_range('yyyy/mm/dd', periods=num, freq='M')
```

"periods=num" specifies the number of the months

'freq='M'' specifies the every month end.

Example 8.5

```
import pandas as pd
result = pd.date_range('2018/06/15', periods=6, freq='M')
print(result)
```

Output:

```
DatetimeIndex(['2018-06-30', '2018-07-31', '2018-08-
31', '2018-09-30', 2018-10-31', '2018-11-30'],
dtype='datetime64[ns]', freq='M')
```

Explanation:

"date_range('2018/06/15', periods=6, freq='M')" returns every month end starting from "2018/06/15", including 6 months end.

Merge DataFrames

We can merge two dataframes together by column name

The syntax to merge two dataframes by column name is:

> pd.merge(dataframeX, dataframeY, on='col_name')

Example 8.6

```
import pandas as pd
X = pd.DataFrame(
        {'ID':[0,1,2,3,4],
        'Name': ['Alva', 'Adam', 'Abel', 'Ally', 'Anne'],
        'Score':[89, 95, 79, 92, 72]})
Y = pd.DataFrame(
        {'ID':[0,1,2,3,4],
        'Name': ['Bart', 'Beth', 'Bush', 'Boyd', 'Bess'],
        'Score':[88, 92, 80, 87, 95]})
result = pd.merge(X, Y, on='ID')
print(result)
```

Output:

	ID	Name_x	Score_x	Name_y	Score_y
0	0	Alva	89	Bart	88
1	1	Adam	95	Beth	92
2	2	Abel	79	Bush	80
3	3	Ally	92	Boyd	87
4	4	Anne	72	Bess	95

Explanation:

"**merge(x, y, on='ID')**" merges dataframe X and dataframe Y together according to "ID".

"ID" is a key to merge two dataframes.

"on=ID" means that two data frames are merged based on the ID.

"Name_x" and "Score_x" comes from dataframe X.

"Name_y" and "Score_y" comes from dataframe Y.

Merge by DataFrame X

We can merge two dataframes by using the key of dataframe X.

The syntax is as follows:

merge(dataframeX, dataframeY, on='col_name', how='left')

"how='left'" means that two dataframes are merged according to the key of the dataframe X.

Example 8.7

```
import pandas as pd

X = pd.DataFrame(

    {'ID':[0,1,2,3,4],

    'Name': ['Alva', 'Adam', 'Abel', 'Ally', 'Anne'],

    'Score':[89, 95, 79, 92, 72]})

Y = pd.DataFrame(

    {'ID':[0,1,2,3,4],

    'Name': ['Bart', 'Beth', 'Bush', 'Boyd', 'Bess'],

    'Score':[88, 92, 80, 87, 95]})

result = pd.merge(X, Y, on='Score', how='left')

print(result)
```

	ID_x	Name_x	Score	ID_y	Name_y
0	0	Alva	89	NaN	NaN
1	1	Adam	95	4.0	Bess
2	2	Abel	79	NaN	NaN
3	3	Ally	92	1.0	Beth
4	4	Anne	72	NaN	NaN

Explanation:

merge(X, Y, on='Score', how='left') merges dataframe X and dataframe Y according to the "Score" of the dataframe X.

The key "Score" of the dataframe X is: 89, 95, 79, 92, 72.

In the output, the merged dataframe only displays the data where two dataframes have the same key. 95 and 92 are the keys that both dataframes have.

If a key exists in dataframe X and does not exist in dataframe Y, then the data in the merged dataframe Y will be NaN.

Merge by DataFrame Y

We can merge two dataframes by using the key of dataframe Y.

The syntax is as follows:

```
merge(dataframeX, dataframeY, on='col_name', how='right')
```

"how='right'" means that two dataframes are merged according to the key of the dataframe Y.

Example 8.8

```python
import pandas as pd
X= pd.DataFrame(
     {'ID':[0,1,2,3,4],
      'Name': ['Alva', 'Adam', 'Abel', 'Ally', 'Anne'],
      'Score': [89, 95, 79, 92, 72]})
Y = pd.DataFrame(
     {'ID':[0,1,2,3,4],
      'Name': ['Bart', 'Beth', 'Bush', 'Boyd', 'Bess'],
      'Score': [88, 92, 80, 87, 95]})
result = pd.merge(X, Y, on='Score', how='right')
print(result)
```

Output:

	ID_x	Name_x	Score	ID_y	Name_y
0	1.0	Adam	95	4	Bess
1	3.0	Ally	92	1	Beth
2	NaN	NaN	88	0	Bart
3	NaN	NaN	80	2	Bush
4	NaN	NaN	87	3	Boyd

Explanation:

"merge(X, Y, on='Score', how='right')" merges dataframe X and dataframe Y according to the "Score" of the dataframe Y.

The key "Score" of the dataframe Y is: 95, 92, 88, 80, 87.

In the output, the merged dataframe only displays the data where two dataframes have the same key. 95 and 92 are the keys that both dataframes have.

If a key exists in dataframe Y and does not exist in dataframe X, then the data in the merged dataframe X will be NaN.

Pandas

Q & A

Questions

Please fill in the correct answer:

01.

import pandas as pd

print(<u>fill in</u>.__version__)   # check Pandas version

A. dataframe

B. series

C. dataset

D. pd

02.

import pandas as pd

data = {

  "Student": ["Anddy", "Billy", "Cindy"],

  "Score": [96, 99, 98]

}

dataset = pd.DataFrame(data)

print(**dataset.<u>fill in</u>[1]**)   # locate the data by the row

A. locate

B. loc

C. lo

D. nothing

03.

```
import pandas as pd

dataset = pd.read_csv('C:\myData\score.csv')

print(dataset.fill in())     # show data in the first 5 rows
```

A. first   B. header   C. head   D. top

04.

```
import pandas as pd

dataset = pd.read_csv('C:\myData\empty.csv')

avg = dataset["Daisy"].fill in ()     # get average data

dataset["Daisy"].fillna( avg, inplace = True )

print(dataset.to_string())
```

A. average

B. avg

C. middle

D. mean

05.

```
import pandas as pd

dataset = pd.read_csv('C:\myData\car.csv')
```

```
print(dataset.fill in())      # get the correlation of data
```

A. correlation

B. correlate

C. corr

D. cor

06.

```
import pandas as pd

dataset = pd.read_json('C:\myData\grade.py')

print (dataset)

print (dataset.fill in())      # get the standard deviation
```

A. standard

B. deviation

C. std

E. dvt

07.

```
import pandas as pd

import numpy as np

dataset=pd.DataFrame(np.random.randn(6,4),

index=[3,5,2,6,1,4],columns=['Beck','Davy', 'Anna', 'Cary'])

result=dataset.fill in(axis=0)

print (result)
```

A. sort_index

B. sort_row

C. sort_dataframe

C. srot_series

08.

```
import pandas as pd

result = pd.fill in('2018/06/15', periods=6)

# get the range of regular date

print(result)
```

A. regular_date

B. date_regular

C. range_date

D. date_range

09.

```
import pandas as pd

data = [ 10, 11, 12 ]

dataset = pd.Series(data,fill in = ["a", "b", "c"])

print(dataset["a"])

print(dataset["b"])

print(dataset["c"])
```

A. label

B. index

C. row

D. column

10.

import pandas as pd

dataset = pd.**fill_in('C:\myData\score.csv')**

read csv file

print(dataset)

A. read_csv

B. read-csv

C. read_file

D. read-file

11.

import pandas as pd

dataset = pd.read_csv('C:\myData\score.csv')

print(dataset.**fill in(7)**)   # show data in the last 5 rows

A. last   B. footer   C. tail   D. bottom

12.

import pandas as pd

dataset = pd.read_csv('C:\myData\empty.csv')

```
mid = dataset["Anddy"].fill in()    # get a middle data

dataset["Anddy"] . fillna( mid, inplace = True )

print(dataset.to_string())
```

A. middle

B. mid

C. mean

D. median

13.
```
import pandas as pd

dataset = pd.read_json('C:\myData\grade.py')

print ("The original date of the Dataframe is:")

print ("The transposed date of the Dataframe is:")

print (dataset.fill in)    # transpose a Dataframe
```

A. Transpose

B. Trans

C. Tr

D. T

14.
```
import pandas as pd

import numpy as np

dataset = pd.Series(np.random.fill in(5))
```

generate 5 random numbers

print (dataset)

A. randn

B. rand

C. ran

D. number

15.

```python
import pandas as pd
import numpy as np
dataset=pd.DataFrame(np.random.randn(6,4),
index=[3,5,2,6,1,4],columns=['Beck','Davy', 'Anna', 'Cary'])
result=dataset.sort_index(fill in)   # sort data by columns
print (result)
```

A. axis=0

B. axis=1

C. col

D. columns

16.

```python
import pandas as pd
result = pd.fill in ('2018/06/15', periods=6)
# get the range of the business date
```

120

print(result)

A. business_range

B. business_date

C. bdate_range

D. range_bdate

17.

dataset.loc[1] will return a _____?

dataset.loc[[1]] will return a _____?

A. NumPy   Pandas

B. Pandas   NumPy

C. DataFrame   Series

D. Series   DataFrame

18.

import pandas as pd

dataset = pd.read_csv('C:\myData\empty.csv')

dataset.<u>fill in</u>(inplace = True)

remove the rows containing NaN values

print(dataset.to_string())

A. removena

B. dropna

C. deletena

D. eradicatena

19.

```
import pandas as pd

dataset = pd.read_csv('C:\myData\empty.csv')

hot = dataset["Anddy"].fill in ()[0]

# get the data that most frequently appears

dataset["Anddy"] . fillna( hot, inplace = True )

print(dataset.to_string())
```

A. frequent

B. freq

C. mode

D. most

20.

```
import pandas as pd

dataset = pd.read_csv('C:\myData\score.csv')

print(dataset.size)

print(dataset.fill in)    # return the number of dimensions

print(dataset.shape)
```

A. number

B. dimension

C. dimen

D. ndim

21.

strip()   Remove space of each string
split()   Split every string using the specified delimiter.
<u>fill in</u>()   Concatenate strings

A. cat

B. concat

C. connect

D. concatenate

22.

import pandas as pd

dataset = pd.read_csv('C:\myData\empty.csv')

dataset.<u>fill in</u>(95, inplace = True)   # fill empty cells

print(dataset.to_string())

A. fillempty

B. fillnan

C. fillnull

D. fillna

23.

```python
import pandas as pd

result = pd.date_range('2018/06/15', periods=6, freq='fill in')

# get range of several weekends

print(result)
```

A. Weekend

B. Week

C. W

D. 7days

24.

```python
import pandas as pd

result = pd.date_range('2018/06/15', periods=6, freq='fill in')

# get range of several month ends

print(result)
```

A. Monthend

B. Month

C. M

D. 30days

Answers

01. D	09. B	17. D
02. B	10. A	18. B
03. C	11. C	19. C
04. D	12. D	20. D
05. C	13. D	21. A
06. C	14. A	22. D
07. A	15. B	23 C
08. D	16. C	24. C

Recommended Books by Ray Yao

(Each Cheat Sheet contains more than 300 examples, more than 300 outputs, and more than 300 explanations.)

Paperback Books by Ray Yao

C# Cheat Sheet

C++ Cheat Sheet

Java Cheat Sheet

JavaScript Cheat Sheet

Php MySql Cheat Sheet

Python Cheat Sheet

Html Css Cheat Sheet

Linux Command Line

C# 100 Q & A

C++ 100 Q & A

Java 100 Q & A

JavaScript 100 Q & A

Php MySql 100 Q & A

Python 100 Q & A

Html Css 100 Q & A

Linux 100 Q & A

C# Examples

C++ Examples

Java Examples

JavaScript Examples

Php MySql Examples

Python Examples

Html Css Examples

Shell Scripting Examples

Advanced C++ in 8 hours

Advanced Java in 8 hours

AngularJs in 8 hours

C# programming

C++ programming

Dart in 8 hours

Django in 8 hours

Erlang in 8 hours

Git Github in 8 hours

Golang in 8 hours

Google Sheets in 8 hours

Haskell in 8 hours

Html Css programming

Java programming

JavaScript programming

JQuery programming

Kotlin in 8 hours

Lua in 8 hours

Matlab in 8 hours

Matplotlib in 8 hours

MySql database

Node.Js in 8 hours

NumPy in 8 hours

Pandas in 8 hours

Perl in 8 hours

Php MySql programming

PowerShell in 8 hours

Python programming

R programming

React.Js in 8 hours

Ruby programming

Rust in 8 hours

Scala in 8 hours

Shell Scripting in 8 hours

Swift in 8 hours

TypeScript in 8 hours

Visual Basic programming

Vue.Js in 8 hours

Xml Json in 8 hours

Made in United States
Troutdale, OR
12/30/2024